WORKBO

REJECTION
EXPOSED

ANTHONY HULSEBUS

ABOUT THIS WORKBOOK

⁓

THE PURPOSE OF THIS WORKBOOK is to help you process and put into practice what you learn in *Rejection Exposed* to defeat the cycle of rejection in your life. Each lesson in this workbook contains:

- A chapter summary
- Study questions that review key concepts from the chapter
- Key scriptures to meditate on for personal growth
- Personalized prayer focused on the chapter topic
- Bonus questions for personal reflection and group discussion
- Answer key in the back for suggested answers to the study questions

The appendix of daily confessions from the Bible will also help to renew your mind and release the power of God's spoken word.

My prayer is that you experience the freedom the heavenly Father's love can bring as you study and implement the principles contained in *Rejection Exposed* by completing this workbook by yourself or with a group.

CHAPTER 1

Summary for "Discerning the Root"

We learned in chapter one that we all have roots in our life—some healthy and some not. We can label our root either *loved* or *rejected*. Rejection, like love, is a spiritual force and it has a spirit behind it, as does love. We all respond to rejection differently and what many people fear the most is rejection. It is important to identify how we respond to people and circumstances in life to identify the work of rejection. We need to know our root and check our fruit. This first chapter introduces us to the idea that we may have the wrong root feeding us and it is not good. Some of us may have a hard time defining rejection since it can take on different forms. Someone once was asked to define pornography. He said that while he could not give a textbook definition, he did say, "I know it when I see it." And so it is with rejection; we all know it when we *feel* it.

Write It Out

1. What are the two functions of a root in our life?

   _____

   _____

2. Why do we fear rejection so much?

   _____

There are four main responses to rejection. Fill in the rest of the statement about each category as it pertains to how each area manifests in our lives.

3. Doubt and fear lead to _____

   _____

4. Anger leads to _____

   _____

5. Withdrawal and self-pity lead to _____

   _____

6. Denial leads to _____

_____

Multiple Choice

7. Rejection is so powerful in our lives because:

   a. God made us weak

   b. We love the praise of others

   c. God made us for love

   d. Rejection is more powerful than love

8. In the example of the famous pop star Michael Jackson what did he fear the most?

   a. Not selling records

   b. Not having privacy

   c. Rejection from his father

   d. His famous brothers

Fill in the Blank

9. When you are *wrongly* hurt by _____, _____ and/or _____, you can embrace *personal* _____ and believe a _____ about your true, God-given _____.

10. Active rejection is intentional or _____ physical actions or _____ intended to _____ us physically, _____ , emotionally and _____.

11. Passive rejection is the _____ of a loved one, normally a parent, or spouse or sometimes a friend, girl/boy friend or someone _____. General _____ from someone who is designed to give you _____, _____ and _____.

12. Which of the four categories of responding to rejection seems to be most prevalent in your life today and why? (There can be several or a mixture, but find the most prevalent one.)

_____

_____

_____

True or False

13. _____ Perceived rejection and passive rejection are the same thing.

14. _____ Rejection only steals from the one rejecting you.

15. _____ Being rejected by a loved one is like making a withdrawal on your spiritual bank account.

16. _____ Rejection and their memories will all heal with time.

Key Scriptures

On the next page, write out the following verses and meditate on them for your personal growth:
- Matthew 7:17–20
- Isaiah 61:1–2

Personal Prayer

"Lord Jesus, I see that you want me to understand the root and source in your Word about the battles that I face. That is why you show us the lives of your saints in the scriptures. Lord I ask you to open the eyes of my heart to understand how rejection is working in my life and how I might receive healing from the wounds of the past and defeat the lies that rejection has told me about you and myself. Lord, I thank you that your love for me and acceptance of me is more powerful than anything life or the devil can throw at me. Thank you for your all sufficient grace that destroys rejection and fills my heart with love."

Additional Personal Reflection or Group Discussion

1. Discuss how a child (or an adult) can learn the difference between not getting what we want and real rejection.
2. Discuss passive versus active rejection and how you might identity the difference.
3. What does rejection steal from us and how does this affect us?
4. What has rejection stolen from you and how is it affecting you today?
5. If comfortable, discuss how you were affected by rejection early in your life and how it's affecting you today.
6. Discuss some real-life, recent examples of feeling rejected and how you reacted. What might you change?
7. Can you think back on times that you *felt* rejected (perceived rejection) but realize now that it was *not* personal but you just took it that way? Why do you think you took it personally?

Use the Space Below for Scriptures and Personal Reflection

CHAPTER 2

Summary for "Exposing the Real Enemy"

We learned in this chapter that satan or Lucifer is a real being that was destroyed in terms of his authority when he was kicked out of heaven and thus suffered rejection from God. He is the force behind rejection and not God but we also learned that man doesn't often discern this force and thus fails to deal with the spiritual reality of a root of rejection. Satan has endured much rejection, because of his rebellion and thus he in turns tries to get us to rebel in order to get rejected time and again. We also learned that Eve perceived being rejected by God and rebelled. He knows a rejected person will always separate himself or herself from God. Satan sowed fear and doubt into Adam and Eve's heart the moment he got them to believe that God had in some way rejected them. He does the same thing to us today.

Write It Out

1. Why is satan/Lucifer successful at getting us to rebel against God?

   _____

   _____

2. How did rejection play a role in Eve's rebellion in the garden of Eden?

   _____

   _____

Multiple Choice

3. Eve, then Adam, perceived rejection from God, what two words describe their *reactive* feelings as a result?

   a. Anger

   b. Lust

   c. Fear

   d. Anxiety

   e. Doubt

   f. Sadness

   g. Hopelessness

4. God created us with many strong desires, but which one is the strongest? To be:

    a. fed   b. comforted   c. loved   d. disciplined   e. heard   f. encouraged

Fill in the Blank

5. When Eve thought that God lied to her, she felt _____.

6. This led to _____ and then _____ to enter her and Adam's heart, which caused them to hide from God and "cover" themselves.

7. When we doubt the love of God or others, fear comes into our lives. Satan often lies to us to get us to doubt. Name two lies you have believed that have resulted in fear in your life?

_____

_____

True or False

8. _____ Satan's rebellion caused him to filled with rejection.

9. _____ Eve believed God rejected her when she found out that satan was allowed to come to earth.

10. _____ Doubt and fear come in our hearts as a result of our own rebellion.

Key Scriptures

Write out the following verses on the next page and meditate on them for your personal growth:

- Isaiah 14:13
- Ezekiel 28:16
- Genesis 3:7-10

Personal Prayer

"Dear Heavenly Father, I see now that satan is the real source of rejection and not you. When I have interpersonal conflicts, help me to understand that though I may feel rejected, I can know that I am battling a spiritual foe and not a physical one. Help me not to make those around me my enemies but to see that I am in a war for truth. The truth is that I am loved and cared for, no matter what humans say or do to make me feel otherwise. Lord, I see that satan wants me to doubt your love and provision for me and to fear that I am alone and on my own. Help me, Lord, to see the truth that I can trust you in every way in all situations, just at Jesus did. Thank you, Father, for help in this area of my life!"

Additional Personal Reflection or Group Discussion

1. What lies have you believed about God or others because you felt they lied to you or held out on you?

2. As a result of rejection, especially from parents, how has fear affected you? What kinds of fear harass you? What rejections are they tied to? (Parental, friends, teachers/coaches, ministers, family members or a spouse?)

3. Do you often turn to the "fear of the Lord" to "keep you clean" or to the love of God to inspire you to holiness? Why or why not?

Use the Space Below for Scriptures and Personal Reflection

_____

_____

_____

_____

_____

_____

_____

_____

_____

_____

_____

_____

_____

_____

_____

_____

_____

CHAPTER 3

Summary for "Rejection and Rebellion"

In Chapter 3 we learned that rejection, either real or perceived, as in the case of Eve, can almost always lead to rebellion. Rejection creates a "spiritual imbalance" or lack of equilibrium. Since God created us to have balance in the area of love and affirmation, we will do whatever we can to "right the wrong" that rejection has created. We also can live with constant fear of rejection, which leads to the fear of man or an inordinate desire for the approval of those around us. This is the root of much rebellion in our life. Cain is the primary example of unchecked *perceived* rejection and the sin it leads to.

Write It Out

1. Why does rejection often lead to rebellion in our lives?

   _____

   _____

2. In the two fictional accounts I gave in chapter 3, how are they the same? How are they different? _____

   _____

   _____

Multiple Choice

3. Cain's first reaction to God when He rejected his offering was:

   a. fear   b. anger   c. self-pity   d. remorse   e. shame   f. condemnation

4. People who struggle with anger after being rejected carry a sense of:

   a. worry   b. anxiety   c. fear   d. injustice   e. condemnation   f. pride

5. Saul rebelled against the command of the Lord in 1 Samuel 15 because he:

    a. was the first king of Israel

    b. hated his father

    c. feared the people and listened to their voice

    d. was depressed

Fill in the Blank

6. Most people sin because they want the _____ of others.

7. When God saw that Cain was angry after he felt rejected, God still cared about him by _____ Cain about the attack of the enemy (Genesis 4: 7).

8. In the Cycle of Rejection in Chapter 3, once we carry an offense and are hurt we focus on our _____ instead of our _____.

True or False

9. _____ The Bible proves there are times when rejection and temptation are too much for us.

10. _____ When we are rejected, we feel out of balance emotionally and will always try to find a way to "right the ship," often times by rebelling and feeding our fleshly nature.

11. _____ Anger issues are almost always tied to rejection issues.

Key Scriptures

Write out the following verses on the next page and meditate on them and even memorize them.

*   Genesis 4:3
*   Romans 8:31
*   1 Peter 2:23–24

Personal Prayer

"Dear Heavenly Father, I see how our first parents believed a lie about you from satan. I see that satan is the one who is trying to get me to rebel against you by lying to me about you. Lord, I thank you that you have not, nor will you ever reject me. You have never withheld anything good from me and when I *feel* rejected by you or when I feel that you have not done what I thought was best, I ask you for the grace to trust you to resist rebellion and not do my own thing to feel better. Help me to be aware of the connection between rejection and rebellion. Thank you, Jesus, for your grace to help in my times of need in this area!"

Additional Personal Reflection or Group Discussion

1. What could have Cain done to resolve his rejection?
2. Does it encourage you to know that God knew how Cain felt and knows how you *feel*?
3. Do you get angry when rejected or does your "countenance fall" and do you get sad, depressed, and tend towards self-pity?
4. How does Jesus' warning in Matthew 5 relate to rejection?
5. Do you carry a sense of being cheated in life, or an injustice? How can you resolve that? How can we help others to whom an injustice has been done?

Use the Space Below for Scriptures and Personal Reflection

_____

_____

_____

_____

_____

_____

_____

_____

_____

_____

_____

_____

_____

_____

_____

_____

_____

_____

_____

_____

_____

_____

_____

_____

_____

_____

_____

_____

_____

_____

_____

_____

_____

_____

_____

_____

_____

_____

CHAPTER 4

Summary for "Rejection and Self-Pity"

We learned in this chapter that being rejected can lead to strong feelings of self-pity, depression, and lethargy. Several of the examples are interesting because Cain was not personally rejected and neither was king Ahab, yet they both took their situations personally and it led to serious sin. We learned that rejection has a "voice" and so does God and scripture. This is because rejection has a spirit behind it. Of course scripture speaks to us because it has a Spirit behind it—the Holy Spirit; Jesus makes this clear in John 6:63. King Ahab is the best biblical example of rejection and self-pity, but we also saw that Cain's reaction to rejection was anger *and* self pity, which can be the case with us too. Ahab is an important person to study for men who could allow "Jezebel" in their life if they let rejection run its course!

Write It Out

1. Why does rejection lend it self to self-pity? _____

    _____

2. When Ahab went in his room and "turned his face away" after being rejected by Naboth, which of the two reactions of withdrawal was he getting into? _____

    _____

Multiple Choice

3. When we feel sorry for ourselves and get into self pity we also tend to:

    a. cry   b. withdraw   c. pray   d. get around others   e. get anxious

4. Self-pity tempts us to be:

    a. angry   b. dishonest   c. weak   d. depressed   e. overweight

5. The best way to avoid withdrawal after rejection is to:

    a. sing   b. communicate   c. be aggressive   d. read the Bible   e. exercise

6. What are the two most common mind-sets that make us withdraw when rejected?

    a. getting even

    b. pursuit to test loved ones

    c. to reject others

    d. out of emotional capacity

Fill in the Blank

7. Ahab's self-pity created a _____ for Jezebel to step into.

8. Saul tried to use _____ to manipulate his people to help him when he was hunting for David.

9. When rejection leads to withdrawal, it never heals us it only _____.

True or False

10. _____ There is rarely a connection between rejection, self-pity, and lust.

11. _____ Those who react to rejection with self-pity will often use it to manipulate others.

12. _____ It is often because we let rejection make us forget who we really are in God's eyes that it leads to self pity.

Key Scriptures

Write out the following verses on the next page and meditate on them for your personal growth.

• Genesis 4:5

• 1 Kings 21:1–4

Personal Prayer

"Heavenly Father, I see how we can go to self-pity when rejected. I also see how we can use self-pity to manipulate others. So I now renounce all manipulation due to self-pity in my life. I also see, Lord, how one can withdraw and run away when rejected, just as King Ahab did. I realize this can be for several reasons and Lord, if I have done this to manipulate, I repent. I ask you to show me when I am hiding from situations due to the fear of the pain of rejection and give me the grace to run *to* the problem, *reject* hiding and withdrawing, and *communicate* with those around me". Thank you, Jesus, for your grace to help in my times of need in this area!"

Additional Personal Reflection or Group Discussion

1. Remember, "rejection steals" and discuss what Cain and Ahab might have felt it "stole" from them.
2. What could they have done to stay away from self-pity and the sin it led to?
3. Reflect on how rejection has led to sexual sin in your life.
4. Reflect on how rejection has led to being manipulated by others or caused you to manipulate others.
5. Reflect on how to identify the two reasons we withdraw when rejected.

Use the Space Below for Scriptures and Personal Reflection

_____

_____

_____

_____

_____

_____

_____

_____

_____

_____

_____

_____

_____

_____

_____

_____

_____

_____

_____

_____

_____

_____

_____

_____

_____

_____

_____

_____

_____

_____

_____

_____

_____

_____

_____

_____

_____

_____

CHAPTER 5

Summary for "Rejection and Spiritual Warfare"

This is the key chapter to help you understand that you and I are in a spirit world and that there is a war going between light and darkness—more specifically love and acceptance versus rejection and fear. Satan is full of rejection because of his rebellion and subsequent expulsion from heaven. Now his goal is to convince you that God has rejected or will reject you. Smaller creatures under satan's control (demons) work for satan to keep people from God. They use rejection to cause people to hate other people and also run from God. Jesus demonstrated the answer for rejection by loving us even to his death.

If you read the gospels, you will see Jesus' victory over demons, and the book of Acts demonstrates Christian's victory over demons. We also learned that because satan is so filled with rejection, the "strong man" Jesus talked about is usually rejection as well. Demons speak to us and when we are wounded, they begin to "train us" and attempt to control our lives. The good news is that no rejection is too powerful for Jesus to heal and restore!

Write It Out

1. Ever since Lucifer was kicked out of heaven, he has had an agenda. What is it and how does he go about it? _____

   _____

   _____

2. How does a demon actually enter our lives and operate (5 step process)?

   _____

   _____

   _____

   _____

   _____

Multiple Choice

3. What are the signs that the level of rejection someone is experiencing is directed by a spirit?

 a. out of control emotions

 b. auto immune disorders

 c. appetite problems

 d. phobias

4. When Jesus spoke of a strongman he was referring to:

 a. Roman governor

 b. a generational demon from your parents

 c. a principality

 d. the ruling demon in a person

Fill in the Blank

5. 2 Corinthians 10 teaches that our _____ is not against _____ and _____ but against _____ and _____.

6. As human beings, we exit 100 percent in the _____ world and the _____ world at the same time.

True or False

7. _____ Demons take on the name of the activity they induce in us.

8. _____ A spirit of rejection will only enter our lives if we reject others.

9. _____ Demon spirits enter our lives if we are hurt/traumatized by others or by our own sin.

Key Scriptures

Write out the following verses on the next page and meditate on them for your personal growth.

- 2 Corinthians 10:1–3
- Matthew 12:43, 44
- Isaiah 61:1–3

Personal Prayer

"Lord Jesus, I acknowledge that I am, as a human, involved in spiritual warfare. So I ask you to reveal to me the spiritual nature of rejection and the truth about the spirit world. Show me how this spirit works in my life and how you would have me experience the victory you won over demons on Calvary. Lord, help me to see what other spirits are working in conjunction with rejection, such as self-pity, shame, condemnation, or whatever you want to show me. Show me who is the strong man in my life and what other spirits are there. But right now, by the authority of Jesus Christ given to me as his child, I command the spirit of rejection to leave me and my family now and forever in Jesus' name!"

Additional Personal Reflection or Group Discussion

1. How have you thought about demons/spirits before reading this chapter?
2. How has your thinking changed?
3. Are you open to the fact that you have allowed a spirit of rejection to rule part of your life?
4. What are some major events of pain and wounding where the spirit of rejection may have gained access?
5. Ask the Lord to show you times of potential demonic access, even from the womb to present.
6. Ask the Lord to give you the grace to forgive those who have rejected you.

Use the Space Below for Scriptures and Personal Reflection

_____

_____

_____

_____

_____

_____

_____

_____

_____

_____

_____

_____

_____

_____

_____

_____

_____

_____

_____

_____

_____

_____

_____

_____

_____

_____

_____

_____

_____

_____

_____

_____

_____

_____

_____

_____

_____

_____

CHAPTER 6

Summary for "Rejection and Insecure Leadership"

In this chapter we examine the effects of rejection in the life of King Saul. While we get into more detail in chapter 7, I discuss the probable source of rejection in Saul's life: passive rejection. His father most likely ignored him, was indifferent, and too busy for his son. This proved to be disastrous when son Saul became King Saul, for Saul was an unloved son, which Proverbs warns is like an earthquake. At first shame was the only manifestation of Saul's rejection, but then it led to open rebellion and a whole life of disobedience. Saul wanted acceptance so badly that he was willing to sin greatly to get it, including murder and sedition.

Write It Out

1. What were some signs or symptoms of King Saul's rejection?

_____

_____

_____

2. How did the fear of man (Proverbs 29:25) manifest itself in the life of Saul?

_____

_____

Multiple Choice

3. One of the side effects or companion spirits that came with rejection in Saul's life was:

    a. fear   b. anger   c. lust   d. anxiety   e. shame

4. How did Saul's rejection in his life manifest in warfare with the Amalekites ?

    a. retreat   b. fear   c. disobedience   d. poor leadership

Fill in the Blank

5. When we carry rejection in our hearts, we can't admit _____.

6. God tried to _____ Saul by _____ over him the word of the Lord through Samuel.

7. The _____ of man caused Saul to _____ the people and _____ to their voice, which caused him to _____ Samuel's command.

True or False

8. _____ When a person who is a slave in their heart gets a promotion, it always breaks the spirit of rejection in their life.

9. _____ Rejection rarely causes us to take things personally but rather causes us to blame others.

10. _____ At the heart of Saul's rejection and ultimately rebellion was his internal search for his father's approval.

Key Scriptures

Write out the following verses on the next page and meditate on them for your personal growth.

- Proverbs 29:25
- Proverbs 30:21–22
- 1 Samuel 15:24

Personal Prayer

"Heavenly Father, I see that I can learn so much from King Saul, especially his desire for the approval of others because he never received the approval he wanted from his father. Right now I ask you to show me your love and approval of me. I thank you that 1 John 3:1 says that I am your child! And John's gospel says you will never cast me out of your family. Lord, I also see the trap of the fear of man, and so right now I renounce the fear of man and instead reverence you and trust you in all things. You are my reputation. I see Saul's insecurity and defensiveness and ask you to help me to be aware how rejection might cause me to be defensive and then controlling. Thank you, Jesus, for loving me and driving out rejection by your love! Amen."

Additional Personal Reflection or Group Discussion

1. What parts of Saul's life do you see in you?
2. We see Saul keeping quiet when rejected. Can you think of times when you did that? Why did you not speak up? How would have things been different? Ask the Lord to show you a situation where you were rejected and didn't speak up and how you can respond now, who to forgive, and what made you weak at that time.

3. We see Saul taking his men's fear personally by the statement, "they were scattering from me." Do you see this in your life? Ask the Lord to show you why you do this and what He wants to speak to you about it and perhaps where this started.

4. How does Proverbs 30 speak to you? Are you still a slave in your heart? Or an unloved woman? Ask the Lord to show you if it applies and how He wants to minister to you. If you are in leadership in your home, work or church, ask the Lord to show you how you may be leading from insecurity and a spirit of slavery versus out of being a child of God.

5. Do you play the blame game? Do you find yourself overly defensive? Note it in Saul's life and ask the Lord to show it to you in your relationships.

6. Do you see any fear of man in your life? Do you struggle with often wanting the approval of others and does it lead to disobedience?

7. Why did Saul not receive the affirmation from being anointed as king?

8. Why did Saul keep silent when rejected in 1 Samuel 10?

9. What could Saul have done to heal his rejection and walk in greater obedience?

10. What is the main thing rejections lead us into? (Hint is in previous question)

11. What did God do to try to help Saul with his rejection?

Use the Space Below for Scriptures and Personal Reflection

_____

_____

_____

_____

_____

_____

_____

_____

_____

_____

_____

_____

CHAPTER 7

Summary for "Passive Rejection"

Saul's life is again a great teacher for us when it comes to the effects of passive rejection in our lives. We examined the boy/king's life with father Kish and what may have caused Saul to be a rejected young man. We saw that he had all the outward appearances to be a king but no inward ones. We know that Kish didn't prepare his son for the famous "donkey trip" where he meets Samuel, and thus showed his passive, at best, fathering. But God also did his best to father Saul through Samuel as He does for us with people in our lives. Saul then followed his father's passivity by being an absent king to Israel. This chapter will show you the subtle yet powerful effect of passive rejection and how it is different than active rejection. It leaves us insecure and aimless, having no sense of anyone being there for us in our lives. Ultimately, passive rejection keeps you from being able to assume your God-given identity. Saul was left insecure, lonely, isolated, and angry for it. Shame covered him as he felt unworthy of his father's time and attention.

Write It Out

1. List some of the effects you saw in Saul's life because of his absent father?

   _____

   _____

2. The lie of passive rejection is that you are on your own. How did Saul manifest this in his kingship?

   _____

   _____

Multiple Choice

3. What would be the best word/phrase to sum up the effect of passive rejection?

   a. no identity   b. insecurity   c. fearful   d. loneliness   e. depression

4. The main love language that helps those who have endured passive rejection is:

    a. acts of service

    b. gifts

    c. words of affirmation

    d. touch

    e. quality time

Fill in the Blank

5. Because Saul had an absent father, he believed he was on his _____ and _____ in his life and kingship.

6. Because Saul believed the lie that he was alone and on his own, he had no spiritual _____ and no close _____ like David did with Saul's son Jonathan.

True or False

7. _____ Active rejection (being physically abused, etc.) is worse than passive rejection.

8. _____ If we don't get the fathering that we need in life early on, God has no way of getting it to us later on in life.

9. _____ One of the worst effects of passive rejection is the lack of identity and direction in your life.

10. _____ Rejection is rarely a generational sin, but rather happens in one person's life at a time.

Key Scriptures

Write out the following verses on the next page and meditate on them for your personal growth.

- 1 Samuel 10:35
- Proverbs 23:7

Personal Prayer

"My Father who is heaven, I thank you that you teach me so much in your Word through the lives of those who have gone before me. They have suffered so I could benefit from their lives. I see how Saul never really knew the affirming love of his earthly father and thus lived a life of insecurity, rejection, and fear. I ask you now to show me how passive rejection has worked in my life. Many times I don't see what I have missed in love and affirmation, but I ask you to reveal it to me. I know there is 'bad fruit' in my life that I do not like and I know that I need a greater revelation of your love. I need to know in a greater way what Saul did not know—that you are here for me always, working for my good, working out your plan for me, and doing all you can do to love me and guide me even when

I don't see it. I open my heart right now, Father, so show me the work of rejection in my life that I won't be a 'slave who has become king.' I know I am a king in your kingdom, but help me be a secure one! Amen."

Additional Personal Reflection or Group Discussion

1. Have you experienced an absent father/mother? If so, what were the effects that it had on your life? Write them down as best you can and ask the Lord to show you how to heal those.
2. What did God do to help "father" Saul?
3. What has God done in your life to father you?
4. Can you see the effects of generational sin in Saul and David and Abraham? What about in your life?
5. What have you learned from Saul's life in this chapter?
6. What can you relate to the most?
7. Have you felt like you too were "on your own" because of rejection?
8. Describe the absent father effects you see in your life and in the church.

Use the Space Below for Scriptures and Personal Reflection

_____

_____

_____

_____

_____

_____

_____

_____

_____

_____

_____

_____

_____

_____

_____

_____

_____

_____

_____

_____

_____

_____

_____

_____

_____

_____

_____

_____

_____

_____

_____

_____

_____

_____

CHAPTER 8

Summary for "The Seven Deadly Fruits of Rejection"

Rejection can lead to rebellion and sin of all kinds. I have made a list of the most common rejection-related sins that I saw in Saul's life, my life, and those I have ministered to over the years. As you read this chapter, you probably found some common ground with certain sins, as we all do. While it may seem simplistic to state that rejection is that root of all these sins, we have to ask ourselves, *What really is my motive when I sin? What is driving me, especially as a Christian?* I asked the question in this chapter, "How would you behave if you knew deep in your heart that you were totally, unconditionally loved?" Do you think Saul felt this way? What about David? How about you? How would it change your life? Rejection deeply rooted in our hearts causes striving for love and trying too hard. That scares people and pushes them away, thus reinforcing the rejection. It's a vicious cycle and one we all need to be free from!

Write It Out

1. Why do we as humans tend to go towards sin when we are rejected?

   _____

   _____

2. Of the seven sins I listed, which one seemed to be the strongest in Saul's life and why?

   _____

   _____

3. Of the seven sins I listed, which one seems to be strongest in your life and why?

   _____

   _____

Multiple Choice

4. Saul tried to get David to marry his daughter and then keep him in his house, and then he tried to kill him. What sin was he manifesting?

   a. selfishness   b. fear   c. control   d. anger   e. jealousy

5. Saul hunted David for almost seventeen years of his life, trying to kill or capture him because he thought David and even his own son, Jonathan, were against him. This is a common manifestation of a person who is marked by rejection. What sin below best fits this concept?

    a. paranoia   b. control   c. self-pity   d. anger   e. jealousy

Fill in the Blank

6. _____ manifested anger when his sacrifice was not accepted by God.

7. In 1 Samuel 22:8 Saul said, "Is there none of you who is _____ for me," which shows that _____ _____ was making him, in his mind, a victim.

8. When the young David began to succeed in war, Saul begans to get _____ and he tried to _____ David just as _____ made Cain _____ Abel. Both are manifestation of _____ as a result of feeling rejected.

True or False

9. _____ Saul was initially very secure in his kingship and it was David who caused him to feel rejected.

10. _____ You can see that Saul's father Kish was an absent father by the fact that on Saul's trip to find the donkeys the servant was the one prepared and not Saul.

11. _____ We almost always gravitate towards sin when rejected because most sin is an effort to make us "look good" to the world's system.

Key Scriptures

Write out the following verses on the next page and meditate on them for your personal growth.
   • 1 Samuel 22:8 (in the NASB preferably)
   • 1 Samuel 18:9

Personal Prayer

"Dear Lord Jesus, you paid such a great price to free me from sin and all its consequences. I now see how rejection can so easily lead to rebellion and many other sins. I ask you now to reveal to me how I am improperly responding to rejection by pleasing my flesh. Help me see how control, anger, jealousy, fear, paranoia, and selfishness are affecting my life and those around me. Help me also to see where this root of rejection has come in and how I can allow you to rid me from all roots of rejection. Lord, your Word says that perfect, mature, complete love casts out fear (1 John 4:18), and so now I let go of the things that I was using to comfort myself and to keep fear away. I embrace more of your love.

Thank you, Father, for healing me and setting me free from turning to the flesh to comfort my heart and for filling me with your love. Amen."

Additional Personal Reflection or Group Discussion

1. What can you learn from Saul's mistakes caused by rejection?
2. What do you see in your life that mirrors Saul's?
3. Do you struggle with self-pity?
4. Do you struggle with the fear of man (too much desire for approval)?
5. If you answered yes to the two questions above, ask the Lord to show you the root wound or rejection that may have led to self-pity and fear of man.
6. Do you see any rebellion in your life that has its root in rejection? If so, ask for forgiveness and ask God to show you the *why*, the *who*, and *how* the rejection has caused the rebellion. Who rejected you, why were you rejected, and how does God want you to heal from this wound/ rejection that causes rebellion?
7. Many of us are Sauls in hiding—rebelling in our lives because of rejection. Which of the seven sins listed are you currently struggling with? Find Bible verses that speak to these sins and find someone to pray with you about them so you can find healing (see James 5:16).
8. Choose each one of the seven sins that result from rejection in a group and discuss personal struggles and victories in that area, past or present.
9. For each sin listed, find a verse that shows how we can overcome that sin or at least what the Bible has to say about that sin. For example, for anger see Ephesians 4:2.

Use the Space Below for Scriptures and Personal Reflection

_____

_____

_____

_____

_____

_____

_____

_____

CHAPTER 9

Summary for W.D.D.D.—What Did David Do?

It's one thing to learn about rejection and how it works—the Bible is full of people who were rejected, failed, and suffered much. But God in His infinite wisdom not only gives us examples of those who were rejected, but also lessons on how some overcame it. We're all looking for answers and there is no better place than scripture. David shows us how to look to God when rejected and how to walk it out. There is a huge contrast between a rejected Saul and a rejected David. Both suffered much, but only David took it to God and went on to be a successful child of God, king, and leader of a nation. You too will have to make the choice between seeking God or looking to man to heal your rejection.

Write It Out

1. What was David's first big example of rejection and how did it affect him? (Hint Psalm 27:10)

   _____

   _____

2. When David was hunted by Saul, he must have felt rejected. Why did his rejection not turn to rebellion? _____

   _____

   _____

Multiple Choice

3. The rejection that affected David the most was the rejection from which of the following?

   a. King Saul

   b. His brother

   c. Jonathan

   d. His father

   e. His wife, Bathsheba

4. Which of the following best describes how David dealt with his life of rejection?

    a. He went vertical

    b. He won battles

    c. He played music

    d. He cried

    e. He got angry

Fill in the Blank

5. When David found Saul in the cave and had the opportunity to kill him, he chose not to because he trusted the _____ to vindicate him.

6. David wrote a great psalm of protection and safety while he was being hunted by Saul. He could do this because he had an _____ perspective.

7. When we are rejected, we could follow David's example and _____ out to God, or Saul's example and blame _____ for our problems. The one you choose will determine your victory in life!

True or False

8. _____ David was not as rejected as Saul was so he ended up being a better king.

9. _____ David's rejection by his father and brothers was the reason he didn't become king for so many years, even though Samuel anointed him as king.

10. _____ David dealt with his rejection in the secret place of God, in the place of worship.

Key Scriptures

Write out the following verses on the next page and meditate on them for your personal growth.

- Psalm 31:1–6
- Psalm 68:5
- Psalm 73:13, 16

Personal Prayer

"Dear Heavenly Father, once again you show me the way to healing and wholeness by providing people's lives to demonstrate your plan for us. David was a rejected man who chose to look to you, Lord, instead of mankind for his healing. Saul, on the other hand, tried to feel better about his life by pursuing the death of David. Help me, Lord, to be more like David and look to you for healing, strength, wholeness, and acceptance. Help me to acknowledge what you say about me in your Word and what you have spoken over my life. Even as David must have hung on to Samuel's prophecy that he would be king, so I too look to your written and spoken word over me to encourage myself in times when I feel alone, rejected, and like giving up. Lord, I agree with David when he said, "The Lord is good to all and His mercy are over all His works" (Psalm 145:9). Thank you, Jesus, for your mercy towards me even when I don't acknowledge it. Amen."

Additional Personal Reflection or Group Discussion

1. David's father seemed to be generally ashamed or dismissive of him—also known as passive rejection. If this was your father's relationship with you, can you see how it affected you? Write down some ways it affects you today.

2. If you have experienced rejection from your father, even if it was passive rejection, what was the "message" you believed about you and life in general? Try to recall specific incidents and recall how it/they affected you.

3. If you had siblings, did you experience rejection from them? Passive or active rejection? How has this affected your life?

4. Have you tried pouring your heart out to God in your pain? Spend some time in Psalms and note how David did it and begin to emulate his pattern. Also note how after he poured his heart out in complaint, he ended with faithful confession of what God *will* do to bless his future. Psalm 13 is a quick, good example. Read also Psalm 22, 31, 34 and 35. (Most of the early Psalms were of David's trials so this is a good place to learn this truth.)

5. Share with one another your life experiences of father rejections and how they affected you.

6. Share sibling rejections that may be still going on and how they are affecting your life today.

7. How have you overcome father rejection and sibling rejection in your lives?

8. Discuss with each other how you seek the Lord and pour out your heart to Him and what He has done to help you.

9. Take time praying for those who have rejected you and for those in the group who continue to experience rejection issues.

Use the Space Below for Scriptures and Personal Reflection

_____

_____

_____

_____

_____

_____

_____

_____

_____

_____

_____

_____

_____

_____

_____

_____

_____

_____

_____

_____

_____

_____

_____

_____

_____

_____

_____

CHAPTER 10

Summary for "W.D.I.D.—What Do I Do?"

In this chapter I offer you some things to do to release the lies of rejection from your life. I hope you are seeing the solutions God offers us in His Word. The number one solution of course is: TRUTH. Remember Jesus said He was truth (John 14:6). Rejection is from satan since he is filled with it as a result of his expulsion from heaven. Acceptance is from Jesus. Although He knew the greatest rejection by becoming sin for us, He has made being a part of His family free and unconditional. The truth (Jesus) and lies (satan—called the "father of lies" in John 8:42) are opposites. We must always keep in mind who (not what) is driving us when we feel rejected. We are at war and satan will use the feeling of rejection as his number one tactic to first separate you from God, and then to separate you from others.

Write It Out

1. Why is perspective so important and how do we get God's perspective?

   _____

   _____

   _____

2. Why is it important to be outwardly focused? What will happen if you are not?

   _____

   _____

   _____

Multiple Choice

3. Jesus was able to handle so much rejection from those around him because:

   a. He was the Son of God

   b. He was anointed by God

   c. He meditated on His Father's love

   d. He was a high priest

4. Jesus can be a merciful and understanding high priest right now because:

   a. He is in heaven

   b. He was tempted in all ways in life

   c. He is a Jew

   d. He was crucified

5. Jesus's strength against rejection came from three areas: the power of words, trust, and:

   a. faith   b. love   c. identity   d. fear of the Lord

Fill in the Blank

6. One of the things the people saw about Jesus was that He was not _____ by what others _____, but taught the way of God in truth (Luke 20:21).

7. The opposite of the fear of God is the _____ of man. Proverbs says it leads to a _____.

8. Luke wrote of Peter and Jesus' first meeting and Peter's reaction to the fish miracle. This reveals that rejection always wants to _____ us from God and man.

9. Instead of going away and separating himself from Peter, Jesus invited Peter to follow Him and fulfill his _____.

True or False

10. _____ One of the greatest thing love teaches us is how to receive.

11. _____ Peter became one of Jesus' chosen leaders because he was the most fearless of the disciples.

12. _____ One of the lies of rejection is that you are alone in how you feel and thus no one can relate.

13. _____ Jesus' greatest example of defeating rejection is written in Peter where it says He "kept entrusting himself to Him who judges righteously."

Key Scriptures

Write out the following verses on the next page and meditate on them for your personal growth.

- 1 Peter 2:22–24
- Numbers 14;8–9
- Luke 5:8–10

Personal Prayer

"Heavenly Father, I know that you can do all things, including delivering me from a mind-set and perspective of rejection. I ask you now to let me see all things concerning me as *you* see them—my past, my present, and my future! I also see that I am to be involved in my healing and deliverance. I repent for my passivity in my deliverance and now agree to pursue you, your Word, your people, your church, and all those you send to me for wisdom and healing. Thank you that you are actively working in my life now, today. I purpose in my heart to no longer focus on my pain and rejection but rather on others. You have called me love others, to serve them, and thus you promised that as I "give, it will be given unto me…good measure!" Thank you Lord for all your precious promises to me. I expect you to deliver me totally to become who you created me to be. Just as Peter went from being fearful of you to being your most trusted leader, I too am being transformed from my natural personality into my kingdom personality! Amen."

Additional Personal Reflection or Group Discussion

1. When thinking of the power of words, can you remember words of rejection that have affected your life?

2. What would the Lord say about those words? Ask Him for verses that speak the truth to counter the rejection lies you heard.

3. How has rejection affected your ability to trust? Can you recall a time where your trust might have been hurt?

4. Now find a verse that counters the affect of that trust. (For example, if your father was never there for you or involved, thus you don't trust that God will be there when you need Him, the counter-truth scripture could be, "I will never leave you or forsake you" (Hebrews 13:8).

5. What do you see in Peter's life that you can relate to? Fear of man? Mistrust? Impulsivity? Denying Jesus sometimes and following Him closely at others?

6. How can affirming our Divine Identity heal us from rejection?

7. What verses would you point to? How do the verses in the gospel of John, chapter 1 tie into this?

8. How should we use the power of words to heal us from rejection?

9. What verses would you point someone to for help in "reversing the word curse" in their life?

10. What can we learn from Peter and trust? What healed Peters heart and allowed him to trust God and for God to trust him? What were signs that Peter had a root of rejection in his life?

11. What areas of trust do you struggle with? How is this area related to a root of rejection in your life?

Use the Space Below for Scriptures and Personal Reflection

_____

_____

_____

_____

_____

_____

_____

_____

_____

_____

_____

_____

_____

_____

_____

_____

_____

_____

_____

_____

_____

_____

CHAPTER 11

Summary for "You Can Do This!"

Now it is time to begin to assume your part in your healing. Now is the time to seek the Lord, His Word, His people, and His church to find what you need to defeat the enemy in your personal life and finish your healing. Remember, Jesus promised to "heal the broken hearted." He will do exactly what He promises, but he wants to be your partner not your enabler. He invites you to engage yourself in what He has already done on the cross and believe what HE says about you, not our parents, friends, family members or anyone else in our life. Faith, in anything, is always a choice and choices can never be forced or they are no choices at all. "Seek and you will find, ask and it will be given, and knock and it will be opened to you" (Luke 11:11–14).

Fill in the Blank

1. Three things you can do to deal with the rejection in your life are be _____, receive _____ _____ and love _____, and seek _____.
2. David _____ who God is and what God _____ of him, speaking a positive word of truth to himself.

Key Scriptures

Identify and write out two key scriptures that you want to speak and act upon as you defeat the spirit of rejection in your life.

-
-

Personal Prayer

Talk to God about what you've learned from this study on rejection. Ask Him to come into every broken area and make you whole. Lastly, thank Him for His great and unending love for you. Then go out and live like you believe it because it's even more true than you perceive right now.

Questions for Personal Reflection or Group Discussion

1. What is the main thing you see in Jesus that kept him free from rejection? Is that what you identify as the main thing that will help you in this season of your life as well?
2. What can you see in your life about your "perspective" about your rejection and pain?

3. Because rejection changes reality and how we should form our identity, when you think of your identity, ask yourself these questions:
   - What words would *I* use to describe myself?
   - What words would *others* use to describe me?
   - What words would *God* use to describe me? The key here is the truth that the words we often use to describe ourselves or how we believe others think about us warp and distort the truth about us. Rejection has caused us to believe many lies about ourselves. Ideally we want our words about us and what we believe others think about us to line up with what our Father in heaven thinks about us.

4. Are you more conscious of how you *perform* in your Christian life or *whose* you are? (Remember salvation was primarily designed to put you in a different family and kingdom, not perfect your performance.)

Use the Space Below for Scriptures and Personal Reflection

_____

_____

_____

_____

_____

_____

_____

_____

_____

_____

_____

_____

_____

_____

_____

CHAPTER 12

Summary for "Confession and Freedom"

God's power is in His *spoken* word. His power is the only power that can save and deliver us. His word is like money sitting in the bank that has never had a withdrawal—inactive until we speak it and then act on it. Jesus defeated temptation by quoting or speaking the word of God. He had enough confidence in those words, spoken thousands of years earlier, to defeat the devil during His incarnation! How much more should we trust these words of God today! Mark 11:22—24 says that whoever SAYS to this mountain "be taken up and cast into the sea" and does not doubt in his heart, but believes that what he SAYS will happen, it will be granted to him. Jesus did not say we should "think about or ponder over," but rather "say" to our mountain.

The purpose of this final workbook chapter is to help you start a habit of confession (agreeing with and saying the same thing as God) and thanksgiving.

Instructions

The last chapter of *Rejection Exposed* leads you through a number of scriptural confessions, giving you actual words to pray. The corresponding scriptures are listed below. However, for this workbook exercise, do the following:

- Look up the scriptures (choose one, a combination, or all of them).
- Write out the *key words* in these scriptures for *you*.
- Turn the scriptures into a prayer for yourself.
- Write out these prayers and revisit them daily if possible—declare them out loud and find victory in them. There's power in speaking the word over your life.

Condemnation and Shame

- Philippians 3:13
- Isaiah 54:4
- Romans 8:1
- 1 John 3:20
- Proverbs 24:16
- 1 John 2:1
- Matthew 10:32
- Romans 1:16

Righteousness and Acceptance

- Titus 3:4–5
- Ephesians 2:8–9
- 2 Corinthians 5:21
- Ephesians 1:6
- Ephesians 2:19
- John 15:14–15
- Isaiah 43:4
- Exodus 19:6
- John 10:27–28
- John 6:29

Rejection and Love

- Hebrews 13:5–6
- 1 John 3:1
- Psalm 27:10
- Leviticus 26:11
- Jeremiah 31:3
- Malachi 2:1
- Malachi 3:1
- John 15:9
- Song of Solomon 2:10
- Jeremiah 20:10
- 2 Chronicles 5:13

Forgiveness and Healing

- Proverbs 28:13
- 1 John 2:1–2
- Mark 11:25
- Luke 6:37
- John 20:23
- James 5:15
- Psalm 32:5.
- 1 John 1:9
- 1 John 2:12

- Colossians 2:13
- Isaiah 38:17
- Micah 7:19
- Jeremiah 31:34
- 2 Chronicles 7:13
- Psalm 86:5
- Isaiah 1:19
- Matthew 9:6
- Psalm 85:1
- Isaiah 33:24
- Psalm 78:37
- 2 Timothy 2:13

Mercy

- Number 14:18
- 1 Kings 8:23
- 1 Chronicles 16:34
- Psalm 5:7
- Psalm 23:6
- Psalm 25:10
- Psalm 31:7
- Psalm 32:10
- Psalm 57:3
- Psalm 59:10
- Psalm 66:20
- Psalm 86:13
- Psalm 89:24

Fear

- 2 Timothy 1:8
- 1 John 4:8
- Joshua 1:10
- Lamentations 3:22–23
- Psalm 112:7
- Proverbs 29:25

Victory and Faith

- John 16:33
- 1 John 5:4
- Romans 12:3
- Matthew 17:20
- 1 John 2:16
- Revelation 12:11
- Romans 10:8
- John 17:3
- Romans 8:37-9

Humility vs. Rebellion/Pride

- 1 Samuel 15:23
- Deuteronomy 21:18
- Proverbs 7:11
- 2 Timothy 2:25
- Ephesians 2:8.9
- 1 Peter 5:5
- Psalm 35:13
- Isaiah 58:5
- Psalm 25:7
- Psalm 10:17
- Isaiah 58:6

Self-Pity

- 1 Thessalonians 5:25
- James 4:17
- Psalm 103:13
- Isaiah 63:9
- Philippians 4:8
- Colossians 3 :1
- Isaiah 26:3
- Galatians 3:13

_____

_____

_____

_____

_____

_____

_____

_____

_____

_____

_____

_____

_____

_____

_____

_____

_____

_____

_____

_____

_____

_____

Addictions

- 1 Corinthians 6:9
- Galatians 5:21
- Jeremiah 31:25
- Proverbs 23:29–35
- Proverbs 20:1
- Ephesians 5:18
- Isaiah 28:7
- Isaiah 5:11
- Proverbs 21:4
- Hosea 4:11
- Isaiah 56:10–12
- Isaiah 5:22–24
- John 8:34

Victory Verses!

- Revelation 1:5
- Galatians 5:24
- Galatians 6:7–8
- Galatians 2:20
- 1 Corinthians 9:27
- Matthew 10:28
- Mark 9:43
- Hebrews 10:26
- James 4:4
- 1 John 2:15
- Romans 3:23
- Philippians 2:13
- 1 Thessalonians 5:24
- 2 Corinthians 1:21
- 1 Corinthians 1:7–8
- Romans 5:17
- Zechariah 4:6
- Romans 6:12
- Romans 6:14

_____
_____
_____
_____
_____
_____
_____
_____
_____
_____
_____
_____
_____
_____
_____
_____
_____
_____
_____

ANSWER KEY

Chapter 1—Discerning the Root

1. Feed us and hold truth/lies. They hold the soil they are planted in, like plants in the natural. Good or bad soil is the condition of the heart. See Mark 4 and the parable of the sower.
2. Because we already live in a rejected state...root of rejection. Those who fear no rejection have no root of it in their lives. Jesus being the best example.
3. Anxiety, paranoia and disassociation.
4. Rejection of others.
5. Shutting down of personal relationship and walking away from God.
6. Isolation and loneliness.
7. C
8. C
9. words, action, indifference, pain, lie, indentity
10. planned, words, damage, spiritually, mentally
11. neglect, close to us, Indifference, love, affirmation, affection
12. your answer—whatever is true at this time
13. F
14. F
15. T
16. F

Chapter 2—Exposing the Real Enemy

1. Because he is good at us believing God has rejected us. Once God has rejected, you have nothing to lose...so just start sinning!
2. She felt rejected and then angry and so to "get back" or to create spiritual equilibrium, she rebelled.
3. Anger and fear (though I mention doubt as creeping in, in the book, it didn't lead to a reaction that the rebellion was tied to- anger and fear did).
4. C
5. rejected
6. rebellion and fear
7. Your answer here.
8. T
9. F
10. T

Chapter 3—Rejection and Rebellion

1. Because we feel out of balance and must right that balance. Thus we take matters into our own hands and rebel against the perceived "controller"—God.
2. Both felt rejected. One was passive the other active rejection.
3. B
4. D
5. C
6. approval
7. warning
8. rights, responses (responsibilities)
9. F
10. T
11. T

Chapter 4—Rejection and Self-Pity

1. Because when rejected, we feel out of control and thus feel like a victim. Victims always give in to self-pity.
2. Hiding and running away (quitting is the close third)
3. withdraw
4. weak
5. communicate
6. B
7. vacuum
8. Self-pity (1 Samuel 22)
9. Delays healing
10. F
11. T
12. T

Chapter 5—Rejection and Spiritual Warfare

1. He wants us to join his rebellion and he uses the spirit of rejection to get us feeling that God has or will reject us to follow him unwittingly.
2. Trauma happens, lies are spoken, lies are believed, the demon attaches to us, the demon and you agree and then the demon sets to train us to do his will.
3. A
4. D
5. struggle, flesh, blood, principalities, demonic rulers
6. Spirit, natural

7. T
8. F
9. T

Chapter 6—Rejection and Insecure Leadership

1. Hides when asked to be anointed king; quiet when others attacked him; threatened by David's success; self-pity, control.
2. He listened to the people in 1 Samuel 15 and didn't obey God's command to destroy Amalek.
3. B
4. C
5. We are wrong
6. encourage/strengthen, prophesying
7. fear, listen, obey, disobey
8. F
9. F
10. T

Chapter 7—Passive Rejection

1. Clueless during search for donkeys, shame and hiding at inauguration, fear of man.
2. Lack of trust of others (David especially), control of Jonathan and military. Paranoia and fear that everyone was against him; 1 Samuel 22–23.
3. A
4. E
5. own, alone
6. mentors, friends
7. F
8. F
9. T
10. F

Chapter 8—Seven Deadly Fruits of Rejection

1. Because we feel when we sin we are in control and rejection makes us feel out of control.
2. Anger, because he felt cheated by the life he had and the choosing of him to be king. He felt angry because he sincerely tried to do his best but was handicapped by the home he grew up in. He sensed he was not prepared for the job and he was right.
3. Your answer
4. C
5. A

6. Cain
7. sorry, self-pity
8. angry (and jealous), kill, anger (rejection), kill, rebellion
9. F
10. T
11. T

Chapter 9—W.D.D.D.—What Did David Do?

1. When Samuel came, Jesse didn't bring David in at first. He felt his parents forsook him (Psalm 27:10).
2. Because David knew God loved him and that God had a plan for his life (because of the prophetic word spoken by Samuel).
3. D
4. A
5. God
6. prophetic
7. cry out, humans/others
8. F
9. F
10. T

Chapter 10—W.D.I.D.—What Do I Do?

1. Because it prevents us from believing lies from the demonic realm. Spend time with God.
2. Because we find fulfillment is ministering to God and others, will be sin conscious if we are not.
3. C
4. B
5. C
6. swayed/intimidated, thought (about him)
7. man, snare
8. separate
9. destiny
10. T
11. F
12. T
13. T

Chapter 11—You Can Do This!

1. aware, God's love, others, help
2. confessed, thinks

www.northfirenet.com